Celebrating Our Faith

Eucharist
Family Guide

Principal Program Consultant
Dr. Jane Marie Osterholt, SP

BROWN-ROA

A Division of Harcourt Brace & Company

The Ad Hoc Committee to Oversee
the Use of the Catechism, National
Conference of Catholic Bishops, has
found this catechetical series, copyright
2000, to be in conformity with the
Catechism of the Catholic Church.

BROWN-ROA
A Division of Harcourt Brace & Company

Our Mission

The primary mission of BROWN-ROA is to provide the Catholic markets
with the highest quality catechetical print and media resources. The content
of these resources reflects the best insights of current theology, methodology,
and pedagogical research. These resources are practical and easy to use,
designed to meet expressed market needs, and written to reflect the
teachings of the Catholic Church.

Photography Credits
Cover: Stained-glass windows at Zimmerman Chapel, United Theological Seminary,
Dayton, Ohio. Photography by Andy Snow Photographics.

Printed in the United States of America
ISBN 0-15-900451-9
10 9 8 7 6 5 4

Celebrating Our Faith

Eucharist
Family Guide

Celebrating
Our Faith

Celebrating Our Faith materials involve families intimately in the preparation of children for the sacraments. You, like the catechist who teaches in a school-like setting, will find this a grace-filled opportunity to learn more about your faith.

Each chapter teaches about a particular part of the Mass and reinforces your child's learning with a Scripture story, an activity, and a prayer.

Child's Book

This special keepsake book contains eight 8-page chapters based on the Order of the Mass.

We Are Invited

We Remember

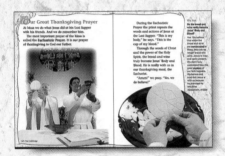

We Celebrate

We Live the Eucharist

Catholic Prayers
Texts of common prayers for children

The Life of Jesus
Summary of key events in Christ's life

Holy Communion
Review of the Church's rules for receiving Holy Communion and the steps for receiving Communion under both forms

Illustrated Glossary
Photographs and descriptions of the people, places, and objects associated with the Sacrament of the Eucharist

Using the Family Guide

The *Family Guide* has been developed to help you prepare your child to celebrate the Sacrament of the Eucharist. No family aid or children's book, no matter how comprehensive, can take the place of your personal witness. You—with your experience, your faith, your commitment—are the best gift you bring to sacramental preparation. As you journey with your child through this sacramental preparation period, adapt the *Family Guide* to suit the needs of your child and to enhance your common experiences of faith.

FEATURES OF THE FAMILY GUIDE

Family Preparation Pages—
lesson plans for use by adult family members to prepare your child for the Sacrament of the Eucharist at home or in neighorhood clusters

Celebrating Other Sacraments—notes for preparing your child for the Sacraments of Initiation

Extra Features—
ways to use the information at the back of the childs' book

Sharing Pages—summarizes each chapter's theme and for use as an ongoing activity (perforated at back of guide)

Note: The *Family Guide* is available in English and Spanish.

My Mass Book
A child's component that can be used at Mass to encourage his or her participation.

Note: *My Mass Book* is available in English or Spanish.

Celebrating Eucharist with Children
Eight 5-minute video segments for classroom or home use

Celebrating Eucharist with Families
Two 40-minute video segments for home use

Celebrating Our Faith Music
A collection of songs from GIA, distributed by BROWN-ROA, suitable for enhancing prayer and liturgy (available on CD or cassette)

HOME LESSON PLANS

Background provides a brief reflection on the doctrinal foundation of the chapter, linked to the *Catechism of the Catholic Church* reference in the *We Ask* feature in the child's book

Getting Started presents various strategies for introducing the chapter content

Sharing the Scriptures opens the Word of God at a level easily understood by your child

Exploring the Liturgy explains and moves your child through the Order of the Mass

More to Share contains follow-up activities related to the larger community your child lives in or worships with and additional books and videos tied to the chapter theme

Living the Eucharist presents activities and prayers geared toward helping your child integrate chapter content into his or her personal preparation for the sacrament

Preparing for the Celebration presents reflection questions that help you look at chapter themes as they are lived out in your own experience

Note: These prayer and meditation times can be used before or after sharing the material in the chapter with your child.

Preparing to Teach a Lesson

Before you begin each chapter:

- read through the two-page lesson plan
- make notes on the steps you would like to adapt
- gather any necessary materials
- preview additional resources you intend to use

Be assured that you are exercising your God-given ministry as your childs' primary teacher. Sharing your faith in this way will be a cherished memory for both you and your child during this time of sacramental preparation.

Celebrating Other Sacraments

This section of the *Family Guide* offers background, suggestions, and resources about preparing children for sacraments other than First Eucharist.

First Communion

Church norms dictate that children of catechetical age (usually second grade) be prepared for First Reconciliation before First Communion. Ideally, preparation for these two sacraments should not be combined, and celebration of First Reconciliation should precede celebration of First Communion.

If you are also preparing your child to celebrate First Reconciliation, you will find BROWN-ROA's *Celebrating Our Faith: Reconciliation* a complete resource.

Confirmation and First Eucharist

Many Catholic communities today are working toward restoring the original order of the Sacraments of Initiation by inviting baptized children to celebrate Confirmation before or at the same time as First Communion.

Because children should be in a state of grace to be confirmed and to receive First Communion, they should ordinarily be prepared to celebrate First Reconciliation before Confirmation and First Communion. Diocesan and pastoral guidelines will shape this sequence, but a general practice would be to celebrate First Reconciliation with a communal service, followed some weeks later by the celebration of Confirmation and First Communion. The Rite of Confirmation indicates that Confirmation of children of catechetical age should be celebrated separately from First Communion and outside a Mass, but you should follow the direction of your diocese.

The Sacraments of Initiation

On occasion children are presented by their families for First Reconciliation/First Communion preparation without the children's having been baptized. If this is your situation you should enroll your child in a children's catechumenate program, where he or she will be prepared to celebrate all three Sacraments of Initiation— Baptism, Confirmation, and First Communion—at the same time (generally at the Easter Vigil, with adult catechumens). If there is no children's catechumenate available to you in your area, you may need to work with one or more members of your pastoral staff to develop a process for your child to be baptised.

In the case of children preparing for initiation, First Reconciliation does *not* precede First Communion. Baptism frees the child from original sin and all personal sin, and Confirmation and First Communion are celebrated at the same ceremony. Children who have celebrated all three Sacraments of Initiation may be prepared subsequently for the Sacrament of Reconciliation and may celebrate this sacrament for the first time at a later parish celebration or individually.

The Order of Initiation

Most twentieth-century Western-Rite Catholics, baptized as infants, celebrated First Communion at the "age of discretion" (sometime around the age of seven) and were confirmed some years later. Not until the revival of the Rite of Christian Initiation of Adults (RCIA), with its profound effects on the way Catholics look at the process of initiation, did most of us ever question the order in which we celebrated the sacraments. Few of us understood that rather than "the way it's always been," the Baptism-First Communion-Confirmation sequence has been the norm for only about a hundred years.

In the early centuries of the Church, initiation (which was most commonly the conversion of adults to Christianity) was understood as a process. The three sacraments —Baptism, Confirmation, and Eucharist—which we now see as separate, were experienced as one continuous movement. The new Christian was bathed in the waters of Baptism, anointed in Confirmation, and invited to the table of the Eucharist in one integral ceremony. This unity is still preserved in Eastern Rite Churches.

The minister of initiation was the bishop, the successor of the apostles and the shepherd of the local Christian community. But as the number of Christians grew, it became more difficult for the bishop to be present to initiate all those wishing to join the faith community. Confirmation and reception of First Communion were deferred until the bishop could get to the widespread parishes. (We still see this today in the practice of celebrating Confirmation once a year at the bishop's annual parish visit.) And as infant Baptism became the more common practice, Confirmation and First Communion were looked on as sacraments of maturity. Full initiation into the Church became a process lasting more than twelve years.

Until the beginning of the twentieth century, however, the original order of the Sacraments of Initiation was still preserved. Children baptized as infants were usually confirmed and invited to the Eucharistic table around the age of twelve or thirteen. It was Pope Pius X, in 1910, who responded to a decline in the number of Catholics receiving Communion regularly by moving the age of First Communion (and First Reconciliation) to the "age of discretion." That decree opened the Eucharist to children, but—with some exceptions, such as the practice in many Latin American Catholic communities—left Confirmation isolated and destroyed the order of initiation.

The theology that sees Confirmation as an adolescent or young-adult rite of passage grew out of this change. In reviving the RCIA and renewing the Rite of Confirmation, the Church left to the discretion of local bishops the minimum age for Confirmation, which led to the situation at the end of the twentieth century, which allowed Confirmation to be celebrated at every possible age from infancy to adulthood.

Scope and Sequence

Celebrating Our Faith
Reconciliation

	Key Theme	Scripture Story	Liturgical Connection	*We Ask* Catechism Reference
Chapter 1 We Belong				
	The Sacraments of Initiation make us part of the Church.	Paul shares the story of salvation (Acts 17:16–34)	Baptism, Confirmation, and Eucharist	*Catechism, #1229–1233*
Chapter 2 We Celebrate God's Love				
	The Sacrament of Reconciliation forgives sins committed after Baptism.	The Forgiving Father (Luke 15:11–32)	Two ways to celebrate Reconciliation	*Catechism, #1855–1857*
Chapter 3 We Hear Good News				
	God's word in the Scriptures reminds us of God's mercy and forgiveness.	The Lost Sheep (Luke 15:1–7)	Welcome and sharing of the Scriptures in the Rite of Penance	*Catechism, #104, 1349*
Chapter 4 We Look at Our Lives				
	We examine our conscience to prepare for confession.	The Ten Commandments, the Great Commandment (Luke 10:25–28)	The examination of conscience	*Catechism, #1777, 1783*
Chapter 5 We Ask Forgiveness				
	We confess our sins and accept a penance.	Zacchaeus (Luke 19:1–10)	Sacramental confession and the giving of a penance	*Catechism, #1455–1456, 1467*
Chapter 6 We Go Forth in Pardon and Peace				
	We pray an Act of Contrition and are absolved.	The Forgiven Woman (Luke 7:36–50)	The Act of Contrition, absolution, and dismissal in the Rite of Penance	*Catechism, #1469*

Scope and Sequence
Celebrating Our Faith
Eucharist

	Key Theme	Scripture Story	Liturgical Connection	*We Ask* Catechism Reference
Chapter 1 Belonging				
	The Sacraments of Initiation make us part of the Church.	Peter's Pentecost preaching *(Acts 2)*	Baptism and Confirmation	*Catechism, #1213*
Chapter 2 Invited to the Table				
	The Eucharist is a Sacrament of Initiation.	The Vine and the Branches *(John 15:1–17)*	First Communion	*Catechism, #1388*
Chapter 3 Gathering to Celebrate				
	We gather at Mass to celebrate the Eucharist.	The early Christians gather for Eucharist *(Acts 2:42–47)*	The Introductory Rites of the Mass	*Catechism, #2180–2182*
Chapter 4 Feasting on God's Word				
	We share God's word at Mass.	The Good Shepherd *(John 10:1–18)*	The Liturgy of the Word	*Catechism, #101–104*
Chapter 5 Offering Our Gifts				
	We offer our gifts to God at Mass.	Loaves and Fish *(John 6:5–13)*	The Presentation of the Gifts	*Catechism, #1366–1368*
Chapter 6 Remembering and Giving Thanks				
	The Mass makes Jesus' sacrifice present.	The Last Supper *(Matthew 26:17–19, 26–28)*	The Eucharistic Prayer	*Catechism, #1333*
Chapter 7 Sharing the Bread of Life				
	We receive Jesus in Holy Communion.	The Bread of Life *(John 6:30–58)*	The Communion Rite at Mass	*Catechism, #1384–1389*
Chapter 8 Going Forth to Love and Serve				
	We have a mission to share God's love with others.	The Journey to Emmaus *(Luke 24:13–35)*	The Concluding Rite of the Mass	*Catechism, #1402–1405*

My First Communion

Help your child fill out this page. Tell your child that by signing the page, he or she is asking the whole parish community to help him or her prepare for his or her First Communion. Sign your name in the box and ask other family members, godparents, prayer partners, and classmates to sign as well.

My First Communion

I will receive
Holy Communion
for the first time
during the celebration of the Eucharist
on

_____

(date)

at

_____

(name of church)

I ask my family, my godparents,
my teacher, my classmates, my friends,
and everyone in my parish community
to help me prepare for this celebration.

_____

(signed)

**Here are the signatures of people who are helping
me prepare for my First Communion.**

A Blessing for Beginnings

"I am the bread that gives life!
No one who comes to me will ever be hungry."

—*John 6:35*

Leader: Today we gather to continue your journey of
　　　　initiation
　　　　as you prepare for First Communion.
　　　　We are ready to learn from one another
　　　　and from our Church community.
　　　　And so we pray:
　　　　God our Father, accept our thanks and praise for
　　　　　your great love.
　　　　Jesus, Son of God, be with us in the Sacrament of
　　　　　the Eucharist.
　　　　Holy Spirit, help us grow as members of the
　　　　　Body of Christ.

Reader: Listen to God's message to us:
　　　　(Read John 6:32–40.)
　　　　The word of the Lord.

All: **Thanks be to God.**

Leader: Let us ask God's blessing on our journey together.

All: **Holy Trinity, lead us to the table of the Eucharist.**
　　　　Teach us to love one another as you love us.
　　　　Help us be living signs of your presence in
　　　　　our midst,
　　　　and lead us to the fullness of your kingdom.
　　　　We pray in the words that Jesus taught us.
　　　　(Pray the Lord's Prayer.)

Leader: May the Lord be with us, now and always.

All: **Amen!**

A Blessing for Beginnings : 5

A Blessing for Beginnings

Use this brief prayer service to begin
your sacramental preparation.
Invite your child's family members,
godparents, and other interested
parishioners to join you for the
celebration.

- To prepare for the prayer service,
choose a reader and provide him
or her with a Bible opened to ***John
6:32–40***. Point out the part of the
prayer service in which the reading
occurs.

- You may wish to play some
instrumental music or sing one
of the songs the children will be
learning for First Communion.

- Take the part of *Leader*. Invite all
present to follow along and respond
together at the parts marked *All*.

- You may wish to include a gesture
of blessing (traditionally, laying
hands on the top of a person's head
or signing him or her with a cross)
to accompany the final blessing.

CHAPTER 1
BELONGING
Pages 6–13

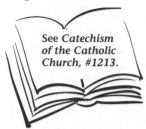

See *Catechism of the Catholic Church, #1213*.

Background The Sacraments of Initiation—Baptism, Confirmation, and Eucharist—make us members of the Catholic Church. Through these sacraments we enter into the Paschal mystery of Jesus' saving life, death, and resurrection. We receive the Holy Spirit and are joined to one another as members of the Body of Christ. It is through Baptism, the first sacrament, that our entrance into the Paschal mystery is made most clear. "Don't you know that all who share in Christ Jesus by being baptized also share in his death? When we were baptized, we died and were buried with Christ. We were baptized, so that we would live a new life, as Christ was raised to life by the glory of God the Father" *(Romans 6:3–4)*.

Preparing Your Child at Home

Getting Started

- Before you begin, talk with your child about what it means to be a member of a group, whether it is a family or an organization. Remind him or her that members share common beliefs and that they help one another. Then help your child write down all of the groups of which he or she is a member. You may want to discuss what is important to him or her about each group.

- After praying the opening prayer and reading the text with your child, point out the pictures on pages 6 and 7. Ask your child how each picture shows belonging. Talk about the similarities between being a member of your family and being a member of your Church family. You may want to share the story of your child's Baptism and discuss how it brought together your extended family with your Church family. Explain to your child what it means to you to belong to your local parish and what it means to be a part of Jesus' Christian family. Point out that the word *Christian*, which is bold-faced in the text, contains the word *Christ* and that *Christ* is another name for Jesus.

Sharing the Scriptures

- Read the Scripture story on pages 8 and 9 with your child. If possible, read it a second time, this time assigning roles for the different characters and acting out the story. When you finish, ask your child who might be telling this story (a child in Jerusalem with his family). Then ask him or her what it might have been like to be that child.

- Ask your child to talk about what is happening in each of the pictures (from the bottom left: Jesus teaching a group of people; Jesus on the cross; the empty tomb signifying Jesus' resurrection; and Peter preaching to the people of Jerusalem). How do the pictures work together to tell Peter's story?

- Explain that Pentecost was originally a Jewish feast day but that Christians celebrate it as the day the apostles received the Holy Spirit from God the Father and Jesus. Ask your child how Peter said others might receive the Holy Spirit (by being baptized). Read the last paragraph with your child again, pointing out that Baptism joins us with the family of Jesus Christ.

Exploring the Liturgy

- Before you begin reading the text on pages 10 and 11, talk with your child about the key words—*Sacrament*, *Initiation*, and *anointed*. Explain that a *sacrament* is a sign of God's grace that makes Jesus present to us in a special way, that an *initiation* is a ceremony by which people are admitted into a group, and that *anointing* is an ancient custom for marking or honoring those people chosen for a special duty. Clarify the term *Sacraments of Initiation* by making out of construction paper or another similar material a "membership" bracelet for each of you. Be creative. The goal is to show the three sacraments—Baptism, Confirmation, and Eucharist—complete in themselves but also combined to make up the Sacraments of Initiation.

- Read the "Baptism and Confirmation" text together with your child. When you have finished, ask him or her to identify the picture that goes with each sacrament and to tell how he or she recognized each one. (The key signs are the water for Baptism and the anointing with oil for Confirmation.)
- Read through the *We Ask* question and answer on the side of page 11. Read slowly, possibly stopping to talk about what each sentence means. You may need to explain that the *Paschal mystery* is another name for the Easter mystery of Jesus' suffering, death, resurrection, and ascension into heaven.

Living the Eucharist

- Read aloud the directions for the activity on page 12. Talk with your child again about groups and initiation and about the Scripture reading from pages 8 and 9. Then allow your child time to complete the exercise. You may want to draw the image of the cross on a separate sheet of paper for yourself so that you and your child can compare and discuss your choices.
- Read "The Grace of Baptism" together. Begin and end by making the Sign of the Cross together. If your child hasn't yet learned it, show him or her that it should be done slowly and with respect. You may want to read the text of the prayer alone and have your child join with you for the "Lord, hear our prayer" refrain. Ask him or her if the refrain sounds like anything from Mass (the response to the general intercessions). Call your child's attention to these words the next time you are at Mass.

More to Share

- Make arrangements to attend a parish Baptism. Afterward, talk with your child about what he or she saw and heard. Tie your experience into your discussions of the chapter.

- *Sharing Page*—Each chapter has its own *Sharing Page*, which is intended to reinforce the chapter's key concepts. Complete the Chapter 1 *Sharing Page* together.
- Books and Videos—You may wish to share these additional resources, available from the library, your diocesan media center, or publishers' catalogs.

For children and families
The Best Day Ever: The Story of Jesus, by Marilyn Lashbrook (Liguori).

Jesus' saving life, death, and resurrection recounted for children.

Celebrating Eucharist with Children (8-part video series) (produced by Salt River Production Group; BROWN-ROA).

Segment 1: Belonging is designed for use with this chapter.

For adults
Catechism of the Catholic Church (CD-ROM) (BROWN-ROA).

The Church's key teachings available in an easy-to-use, multilingual CD-ROM format.

"What Catholics Believe: A Popular Overview of Catholic Teaching," by Leonard Foley OFM (*Catholic Update*; St. Anthony Messenger Press).

Preparing for the Celebration

Read
"Baptism is God's most magnificent gift."
—*Saint Gregory of Nazianzus*

Reflect
What does the gift of Baptism mean to me? How do I show my thanks for God's great gift in my everyday life?

Pray
Generous God,
your gifts of love and grace are all around me.
Help me show my thanks by the way I live.
Guide me as I help my child prepare
to celebrate the fullness of Baptism
at the table of the Eucharist.
Amen.

Chapter 2
Invited to the Table
Pages 14–21

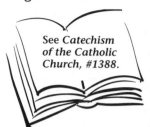

See *Catechism of the Catholic Church, #1388.*

Background The Sacraments of Initiation— Baptism, Confirmation, and Eucharist—are the foundations of Christian life. The new life we receive in Baptism is strengthened in Confirmation and nourished in the Eucharist. But unlike Baptism and Confirmation, the Eucharist may be celebrated over and over again throughout our lives. It is a continued source of spiritual nourishment for our journey. The celebration of First Communion marks the beginning of the initiate's full participation in Christian life, of which the Eucharist is, as the Church reminds us, "the source and summit" *(Dogmatic Constitution on the Church, #11).* So we are encouraged to receive Communion as often as possible.

Preparing Your Child at Home

Getting Started

- Pages 14 and 15 focus on the sharing of our Catholic meal, the Eucharist. Begin by asking your child if he or she can think of any special meals your family celebrates. List these meals on paper, and have your child explain what is special about each one.

- Pray the opening prayer, and read the text with your child. Point out the connection between the text and the photographs. You may wish to highlight the ideas of shared celebrations, meals, family, community, and Holy Communion.

- Have your child point to the two bold-faced terms (*Eucharist* and *Holy Communion*) and talk about them. Explain that the *Eucharist* is the name given to the celebration as a whole, while *Holy Communion* is the specific act of receiving Jesus in the sacred Bread and Wine.

Sharing the Scriptures

- Use the illustration on pages 16 and 17 to identify Jesus and his friends, and ask your child to point out the vine, the branches, and the fruit (the grapes). You may want to read this passage outside, weather permitting, especially if you have access to a grapevine. If you don't, you might point to the trunk, branches, and leaves of a tree or bush.

- Read the Scripture story on these pages.

- Talk with your child about why Jesus told the story of the grapevine. Explain that he was trying to show his friends that he would always be close to them and that, if they continued to live as he taught them, he would nurture them.

Exploring the Liturgy

- Read together the text on pages 18 and 19. Remind your child that the Eucharist, or First Communion, is one of the three Sacraments of Initiation. (You can refer to the membership bracelet from Chapter 1.) If your child has already celebrated Confirmation, explain that this is the final step to full membership in the Church. You may also want to reread the second and third paragraphs on page 19 so your child has a clear understanding of the different ways people are initiated. If you know someone who celebrated all three sacraments at once, you can use him or her as an example.

- Study the two pictures of Communion. If your child is unfamiliar with the ritual of receiving Communion, point out to him or her how the people are holding their hands (cupped one within the other) to receive the Host. Ask your child to point to the bold-faced term *(Body of Christ)*; talk about why we use that phrase to describe the Host. (Explain that just as Jesus gave himself to his friends at the Last Supper, he gives himself to us in the Eucharist.)

- Read together through the *We Ask* column on the side of page 19. Remind your child that First Communion is just the first step in a lifelong process of receiving Jesus in the Eucharist. Draw attention to the photograph on page 18 that shows a First Communion scene. If you see potential similarities to your child's special day, you can point those out.

- *My Mass Book*—Have your child fill out the personalization page of his or her Mass booklet.

Living the Eucharist

- Help your child complete the exercise on page 20 of the textbook. Read the directions aloud, and remind your child about his or her responses to your discussions of special meals and First Communion and of the Scripture story you shared. Write out your answer on a separate sheet of paper and, after you each have finished, discuss your letters.

- Pray together the prayer on page 21. Begin and end by making the Sign of the Cross. This would be a good opportunity to draw your child's attention to the Glory to God prayer during Mass (see page 4 of *My Mass Book*). Help him or her identify the refrain used in this prayer service when you sing or pray the Glory to God at Mass.

More to Share

- Explore ways individual cultures celebrate special meals. If you have access to the Internet or to an encyclopedia on CD-ROM, search for pictures, songs, or movies from different celebrations. Or look together in your local library for similar photos, music, and movies. Look at specific symbols used in the celebrations. Kwanzaa, for example, is an African American feast that uses a seven-stick candelabra called a *kinara* to symbolize Kwanzaa's seven principles. Other cultures enjoy special holiday foods, such as Jewish matzo and blintzes, Irish soda bread, Italian pasta, and Vietnamese *thit nuong* (tit•NUNG)—barbecued meat on a stick. If your family has a symbolic meal or food, make a simplified version of it together.

- *Sharing Page*—Complete the Chapter 2 *Sharing Page* together.

- Books and Videos—You may wish to share these additional resources, available from the library, your diocesan media center, or publishers' catalogs.

For children and families
Celebrating Eucharist with Children (8-part video series) (produced by Salt River Production Group; BROWN-ROA).
    Segment 2: Invited to the Table is designed for use with this chapter.
Grandma's Bread (video) (Franciscan Communications/St. Anthony Messenger Press).
    Mario learns about bread, First Communion, and the meaning of family.

For adults
Celebrating Eucharist with Families (2-part video series) (produced by Salt River Production Group; BROWN-ROA).
    Father Joe Kempf leads a guided meditation on the meaning of the Eucharist.
"First Communion: Joining the Family Table," by Carol Luebering (*Catholic Update*; St. Anthony Messenger Press).

Preparing for the Celebration
Read
"The Eucharist is the means by which we who once received the Spirit in Baptism are constantly renewed in the Spirit until our life's end."
          —*Alan Richardson*

Reflect
How do I experience the Eucharist as a Sacrament of Initiation?
How can I take greater advantage of the blessings offered to me in Holy Communion?

Pray
Holy Trinity,
you have called me to yourself in water and Spirit
and have fed me at the table of the Eucharist.
As I prepare my child for the First Communion,
keep me always open to your invitation
to renew my life and my faith
at the Eucharistic banquet.
Amen.

CHAPTER 3
GATHERING TO CELEBRATE
Pages 22–29

See Catechism of the Catholic Church, #2180–2182.

Background

Participation in the Sunday celebration of the Eucharist is a sign of our Catholic faith. The obligation to participate in the Mass each week is not merely a duty, but a compelling reminder of how deeply the Eucharist shapes our identity. The parish community gathers to celebrate in liturgy what it is in life: the Body of Christ. During the Introductory Rites of the Mass, we sing, pray, and recall God's mercy. In our gathering as the Eucharistic assembly, presided over by the priest and served by the other liturgical ministers, Christ is truly present. "Whenever two or three of you come together in my name, I am there with you" (Matthew 18:20).

Preparing Your Child at Home

Getting Started

- Pray the opening prayer, and read the text on page 22 with your child. Before moving on to page 23, answer the question "What are some things you like to do when you get together with family members and friends?" Remind your child about the concept of community as you talk. Community can mean the actual group of people gathered together or the feeling one gets from being a member of that group.

- Finish reading the text on page 23. Make the connection for your child between the words *parish* and *community*. Explain that we use the word *parish* to describe our Church community, but that our community can actually be much larger—made up of neighbors, friends, and classmates. Now ask the question from page 22 in a different way. Ask what you enjoy doing with members of your parish community. The text gives the example of singing. Talk about some other examples.

Sharing the Scriptures

- Read together the Scripture story on pages 24 and 25. Talk about what it must have been like to be members of the first Christian communities. They often met in homes to share the good news of Jesus.

- Ask whether your child notices any similarities between how the first Christians celebrated and how we celebrate today. (Some possible answers are that they gather together to celebrate Jesus and to worship God, they sing, they share the Eucharist, they ask forgiveness from one another, they pray, and they share their money with one another.)

- Talk together about the illustration. What kinds of things can you see that suggest a community? There are many answers that will fit. You can point out that the people are sharing a meal (the dishes at the bottom of the picture are most likely where the bread and wine are being kept) or that they have similar beliefs and interests.

Exploring the Liturgy

- Before you begin reading pages 26 and 27, go over the bold-faced terms with your child. The terms are defined within their sentences, so it may just be a matter of reading the sentence and then asking the child to give you a definition in his or her own words. You can also look over the pictures (especially the photo on page 26) and identify key images. Point to the procession as a whole, to the priest and deacon, to the large book (called the *Lectionary*), or the processional cross being carried by one of the servers.

- Read the text of "The Mass Begins" on pages 26 and 27. The section on the Sign of the Cross can give you and your child a chance to review this gesture together. When you've finished, read together the *We Ask* question and answer. Talk about what the word *duty* means to each of you and why the celebration of the Eucharist is a duty. (You may suggest it's because it keeps us close to Jesus and to one another.)

- *My Mass Book*—Allow your child time to complete pages 2–4. You may want to play some relaxing music for him or her. You can review the pages with your child either now or when you go through the chapter's *Sharing Page*.

Living the Eucharist

- Read aloud the directions for the exercise on page 28. If you don't want to cut up family pictures, you can help your child write down each person's given name or family name. Point out to your child that the parish community will be uniting to celebrate his or her special day.

- Pray together the Lord, Have Mercy on page 29. Tell your child that this prayer is a form of the prayer sometimes used in the Penitential Rite at Mass. Begin and end with the Sign of the Cross.

More to Share

- If you have the time and materials, have your child create a door banner for your home. The banner can include the name of the parish, symbols of what you, as a parish, share with one another, and the names of your family members.

- Volunteer an hour or two of your time to work on a community-building project. If nothing is available, or if, for some reason, this is not an option, volunteer to be a greeter with your child at this week's Mass. The idea is to make your child more aware of the community around him or her.

- *Sharing Page*—Complete the Chapter 3 *Sharing Page* together.

- Books and Videos—You may wish to share these additional resources, available from the library, your diocesan media center, or publishers' catalogs.

For children and families

Celebrating Eucharist with Children (8-part video series) (produced by Salt River Production Group; BROWN-ROA).

Segment 3: Gathering to Celebrate is designed for use with this chapter.

My Father's House (video) (Franciscan Communications/St. Anthony Messenger Press).

A child preparing for First Communion tours a traditional Catholic church.

Sunday Morning, by Gail Ramshaw (Liturgical Training Publications).

The parish community gathers for Mass.

A Walk Through Our Church, by Gertrud Mueller Nelson (Paulist Press).

An illustrated tour of the objects, people, and actions associated with the life of a parish.

For adults

"How All of Us Celebrate the Mass," by Sandra de Gidio OSM (*Catholic Update*; St. Anthony Messenger Press).

Preparing for the Celebration

Read

"It is a law of our nature, written into our very essence, that we should want to stand together with others in order to acknowledge our common dependence on God, our Father and Creator."

—*Thomas Merton*

Reflect

What do I treasure most about the opportunity to gather with others for liturgy? Where do I see Christ present in my parish community?

Pray

Welcoming God,
you rewarded the hospitality of Sarah and Abraham with your covenant of love.
Open my eyes to all those who need welcoming in your name.
Be with me and my child
as we prepare for the Eucharistic celebration,
as you are with us always in the assembly of your people.
Amen.

CHAPTER 4
FEASTING ON GOD'S WORD
Pages 30–37

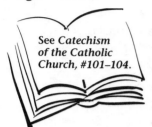

See Catechism of the Catholic Church, #101–104.

Background As Catholics our attitude toward the Scriptures is one of profound respect and living devotion. The inspired word of God is alive in our midst, and its good news is fresh in every time and place. That is why the breaking open and sharing of God's word is such an important part of our liturgical celebration. Christ, the Word of God, is present in the Scriptures as he is in the sacred Bread and Wine. The Mass invites us to be nourished at one table, where the word and the Eucharist are our feast. And then we are sent out into the world to carry the good news to others, to touch their lives as the word of God has touched ours. "The Word that gives life was from the beginning, and this is the one our message is about. Our ears have heard, our own eyes have seen, and our hands touched this Word" *(1 John 1:1).*

Preparing Your Child at Home

Getting Started

- Before you begin the chapter, share with each other your favorite stories (preferably not from the Bible). They can be ones that you have read or heard, but you should each retell a story from memory. It's not necessary that you get very detailed. The focus should be simply on the message of the story. What was it about that particular story that affected you more than a similar story? Talk about an image or two that stood out when you first heard or read the story.

- Now pray the opening prayer, and read the text on pages 30 and 31 with your child. Tell him or her that *Scripture* is another word for the stories of the Bible. Compare the photos on the two pages and talk about how, in each of the scenes, a group (the family group and the Church group) is sharing a story.

- Provide a Bible for yourself and your child. (The version used in your child's book is the *Contemporary English Version,* sometimes called *The Bible for Today's Family.* It is an easy-to-understand translation in everyday language.) Point out the difference to your child between the Old and New Testaments. Explain that the Old Testament contains the stories of God's people before Jesus and that the New Testament contains the stories of Jesus and his disciples. Take turns thumbing through and naming various books in your Bible. You might highlight a few of the more commonly referred to books, such as Genesis, Psalms, the Gospels, or the Acts of the Apostles.

Sharing the Scriptures

- Ask your child if he or she knows what a shepherd's job is. If not, look for resources on the Internet or at your library that may help illustrate the job of a shepherd.

- Read the story of "Jesus, the Good Shepherd" on pages 32 and 33. Talk about the story and the illustration on the page. Ask your child how Jesus is like a shepherd. Possible answers are that Jesus saved us by giving his life, that he loves us all unconditionally, or that he has a special concern for those who are weak or ill.

- Tell your child that the word *pastor,* the title of the priest in charge of your parish, means "shepherd." Draw the connection to your own parish by asking your child what your pastor does to take care of his people.

Exploring the Liturgy

- Clarify the bold-faced terms with your child before you read the entire selection. Explain that the *Liturgy of the Word* is the first great part of the Mass, during which we read stories from Scripture. We use the Hebrew word *Alleluia,* which means "praise God," to show how happy we are to hear God's word. The last bold-faced word, *Creed,* is another way of saying "a collection of beliefs." After your child feels comfortable with the words, read pages 34 and 35 together, including the *We Ask* section on the side of page 35.

- When you finish reading, look at the two photographs. Identify the photo on page 34 as a deacon and three servers. The deacon is holding the *Book of the Gospels*, the book that contains the gospel readings used at Mass, and the server closest to him is holding incense to honor the word of God contained in the book. The priest on page 35 is shown giving his homily. Ask your child if he or she recognizes these two scenes from Mass.
- *My Mass Book*—Allow your child time to complete pages 5–7. You may want to play some relaxing music for him or her. You can review the pages with your child either now or when you go through the chapter's *Sharing Page*. As you go through the pages, draw comparisons to your child's own experiences at Mass.

Living the Eucharist

- Read aloud the directions to the exercise on page 36. Discuss Scripture stories your child may know. Allow your child time to complete his or her drawing or story. You may also want to draw or write your own favorite story so that you and your child can share with each other.
- Read the prayer on page 37 together. Begin and end with the Sign of the Cross. You may choose to read the text to your child and have him or her join with you for the responsorial text.
- Notice that the prayer is based on Psalm 23. With your Bibles, show your child how to look up this prayer in the Book of Psalms in the Old Testament.

More to Share

- Ask your child, "If Jesus were to tell you a story right now, which story would you like to hear and why?" Or if your child may not remember many Bible stories, ask him or her, "If you could tell Jesus one story, what would it be? Why?"
- Each of you can design a bookmark that illustrates your favorite story (scriptural or not). You may choose to illustrate it with an image, scene, or quote from your story. When you're finished, share your design with each other. You may even choose to laminate them. Office supply stores often have iron-on lamination. Place your new bookmarks in your Bible.
- *Sharing Page*—Complete the Chapter 4 *Sharing Page* together.
- Books and Videos—You may wish to share these additional resources, available from the library, your diocesan media center, or publishers' catalogs.

For children and families

Celebrating Eucharist with Children (8-part video series) (produced by Salt River Production Group; BROWN-ROA).

Segment 4: Feasting on God's Word is designed for use with this chapter.

The Lord Is My Shepherd: The 23rd Psalm, by Tasha Tudor (Philomel Books).

A beautifully illustrated version of the beloved psalm for children.

For adults

"The Creed: Faith Essentials for Catholics," by Thomas Bokenkotter (*Catholic Update*; St. Anthony Messenger Press).

How to Read and Pray the Gospel (Liguori).

A handbook for living God's word every day.

Preparing for the Celebration

Read

"Divine Scripture is a feast of widsom, and the single books are the various dishes."

—Saint Ambrose

Reflect

How am I nourished by reading, hearing, and reflecting on God's word in the Scriptures? Which of the "various dishes"—the individual books of the Bible—gives me the most spiritual nourishment? Which books do I need to "taste" more of?

Pray

God of wisdom,
you have graciously shared your living word
　　with me.
Let me continue to be nourished by the Scriptures
as I help my child break open and share the
feast of your good news.
Amen.

CHAPTER 5
OFFERING OUR GIFTS
Pages 38–45

See *Catechism of the Catholic Church, #1366–1368.*

Background Our belief in the sacrificial nature of the Mass has been downplayed in recent years perhaps because this dimension had been overly stressed in earlier times. Two thousand years after the time of Christ, we are out of touch with the idea of sacrifice as a religious ritual, and language that includes words such as victim and atonement makes us uncomfortable. But the true meaning of Christ's sacrifice has never changed. To offer oneself as a sacrifice—as Jesus did on the cross, as we are called to do at every Mass—is to give oneself wholeheartedly, lovingly, and freely to a holy purpose. "God was pleased for him to make peace by sacrificing his blood on the cross, so that all beings in heaven and on earth would be brought back to God" *(Colossians 1:20).*

Preparing Your Child at Home

Getting Started

- Often when families get together, certain members are responsible for bringing specific items. (For example, Grandma brings the dessert; an uncle or cousin brings the vegetables.) If this is the case in your family, ask your child to tell you who brings what. Or if it is not, ask your child for one thing he or she would like to bring to a special meal.

- Read aloud the opening prayer and the text on pages 38 and 39. Afterward look at the pictures on the two pages. Talk about the connection between the family preparing the meal on the left and the Catholic family meal on the right. You can mention the idea of a special meal, or of sharing, or (if the mother and daughter are making the food to bring to a meal) the idea of a gift of food.

Sharing the Scriptures

- If you and your child have ever gone on a picnic, talk about what you each enjoyed. If possible, consider studying this section or this chapter while on a picnic. It doesn't have to be outdoors. Go to a museum, or even move the furniture out of the way and throw down a blanket in your living room. Like the mother and child in the previous section, make some snacks together to take along.

- Look at the illustration on pages 40 and 41, and point out Jesus, the boy holding the basket, and the crowd of people gathered for the picnic. Ask your child how much food the boy has in his basket and how much it would take to feed the crowd behind them. Read the story of "The Wonderful Picnic."

- Talk together about how the story helps show the importance of sharing during special meals and how nice it must have been to have a picnic with so many friends.

Exploring the Liturgy

- Remind your child about the *Liturgy of the Word* you studied in the last chapter, and explain that the second great part of the Mass is called the *Liturgy of the Eucharist.* Here we offer our gifts to God, and we receive Jesus in Holy Communion in the form of the sacred Bread and Wine.

- Read the text on pages 42 and 43 (including the *We Ask* section), clarifying the bold-faced words before you begin. Discuss what is happening in each picture. (The gifts are being brought forth, and the collection is being taken.) Make a connection for your child to the Mass he or she attends.

- *My Mass Book*—Allow your child time to complete page 8. You may want to play some relaxing music for him or her. You can review the page with your child either now or when you go through the chapter's *Sharing Page.* As you go through the page, draw comparisons to your child's own experiences at Mass.

Living the Eucharist

- Read aloud the directions for the activity on page 44. Talk with your child again about the Scripture story from pages 40 and 41 and about how the members of your family share their gifts. Then allow your child time to complete the exercise. You may want to duplicate the image of the bread and fish on a separate sheet of paper for yourself so that you and your child can compare and discuss your choices.

- Read "Through Your Goodness." Begin and end by making the Sign of the Cross. You may choose to read the text of the prayer to your child and then ask your child to join with you for the response. Draw his or her attention to this prayer during the Liturgy of the Eucharist the next time you are at Mass.

More to Share

- Part of this chapter discussed the presentation of the gifts. Find out how your parish chooses its presenters (often it is open to any congregation member who asks), and volunteer yourself and your child for a Mass in the near future.

- Help your child make dinner for the family. You will, of course, most likely do the majority of the work, but give him or her ownership of the meal. Allow your child to present the meal to the rest of your family. Let him or her experience both the work involved in making a meal and the reward of having completed it.

- *Sharing Page*—Complete the Chapter 5 *Sharing Page* together.

- Books and Videos—You may wish to share these additional resources, available from the library, your diocesan media center, or publishers' catalogs.

For children and families

The Boy Who Gave His Lunch Away, by Dave Hill (Concordia Press).

Jesus' Big Picnic (Concordia Press).

Two versions of the miracle of the loaves and fish retold for children.

Bread Is for Eating, by David and Phyllis Gershafor (Henry Holt and Co., Inc.).

A story about making and sharing bread is accompanied by a traditional Hispanic folk song.

Celebrating Eucharist with Children (8-part video series) (produced by Salt River Production Group; BROWN-ROA).

Segment 5: Offering Our Gifts is designed for use with this chapter.

Loaves of Fun: A History of Bread with Activities and Recipes from Around the World, by Elizabeth M. Harbison (Chicago Review Press).

Let's Say Grace: Mealtime Prayers for Family Occasions Throughout the Year, by Robert M. Hamma (Ave Maria Press).

For adults

Babette's Feast (video) (Liturgy Training Publications).

This feature film is a beautiful parable about sharing food and life.

Preparing for the Celebration

Read

"We must not only give what we have; we must also give what we are."

—D. Joseph Mercier

Reflect

What sacrifices am I called to make for the sake of others?

What gifts has God given me to share?

Pray

Jesus,
you gave your life for us
with complete freedom and love.
Teach me to give of myself
ungrudgingly and without keeping score.
Help me guide my child
to a life of unselfish openness.
Amen.

CHAPTER 6
REMEMBERING AND GIVING THANKS
Pages 46–53

See Catechism of the Catholic Church, #1333.

Background The Eucharistic Prayer of the Mass is our great prayer of praise and thanksgiving, calling to mind God's saving actions in the Passover and in the great sacrificial offering of Jesus' death and resurrection. In the Eucharistic Prayer the love story of salvation reaches its fulfillment. Using the words of Jesus at his Last Supper, the priest consecrates the bread and wine. By the power of the Holy Spirit, they become the Body and Blood of Christ, truly present. In this celebration we do as Jesus commanded when he told his apostles, "Eat this and remember me. . . . Drink this and remember me" *(1 Corinthians 11:24–25).*

Preparing Your Child at Home

Getting Started

- Point out that the bold-faced word on page 47, *Eucharist,* means "thanksgiving." Talk together about some things your family is thankful for. Compare the two photographs that show "thanksgiving." Ask your child what is similar about our Church thanksgiving and our family thanksgiving. (We gather around a table, we share food, we pray, we share the day with others, or we recognize all the good things that have happened to us.)

- Pray together the opening prayer, and read the text on pages 46 and 47.

Sharing the Scriptures

- Share the story of the Last Supper on pages 48 and 49.

- Talk about the illustrations. Ask your child if he or she knows what the top picture depicts. (Moses leading the Israelites out of Egypt.)

- Develop a script of what you think took place during the Last Supper. Use the text for guidance. Play out your script, using flatbread, such as pita or matzo, and grape juice.

Exploring the Liturgy

- Ask your child to read and tell you about each of the bold-faced words on pages 50 and 51, including those in the *We Ask* text. Clarify any terms that he or she does not understand. In a missalette, find a copy of one of the Eucharistic Prayers used at Mass, and read it to your child. Explain that the word *consecrated* means "to make sacred"; here, more specifically, it means that the consecrated Bread and Wine are the Body and Blood of Jesus.

- Now, read the complete text of "Our Great Thanksgiving Prayer" and *We Ask* with your child. Draw comparisons to the Mass as celebrated in your parish to help your child better understand this section in context.

- *My Mass Book*—Allow your child time to complete pages 9–11. You may want to play some relaxing music for him or her. You can review the pages with your child either now or when you go through the chapter's *Sharing Page.* As you go through the pages, draw comparisons to your child's own experiences at Mass.

Living the Eucharist

- Read through the directions for the activity on page 52. Remind your child about ways we give thanks and some things for which we are thankful. Allow enough time to complete the two prayers. While he or she is finishing, you can complete your own set of prayers so that the two of you can share your responses.

- Pray the "We Give Thanks" prayer together. Begin and end with the Sign of the Cross. You may choose to read the prayer text yourself and invite your child to join with you for the response.

More to Share

- Try to arrange a time to take your child through the church building at a time other than the normal celebration of Mass. Some older-style churches still have a fully separate altar. Explain that this altar is used as an altar of repose, holding the tabernacle where consecrated Hosts are kept. Take time to look at the stained-glass windows, the stations of the cross, the statues and paintings—anything that your child may overlook or take for granted.

- Pull out old photo albums of holidays during which you give thanks. Pictures of Christmas with presents may give your child a more concrete feel for the ideas of gifts and thanks we have been discussing.

- *Sharing Page*—Complete the Chapter 6 *Sharing Page* together.

- Books and Videos—You may wish to share these additional resources, available from the library, your diocesan media center, or publishers' catalogs.

For children and families

Bread and Wine: The Story of the Last Supper, by Denise Ahern (Concordia Press).

   The events of Jesus' Last Supper retold for children.

Celebrating Eucharist with Children (8-part video series) (produced by Salt River Production Group; BROWN-ROA).

   Segment 6: Remembering and Giving Thanks is designed for use with this chapter.

The Last Supper (video) (produced by Ark Enterprises; BROWN-ROA).

   The institution of the Eucharist is dramatized.

For adults

"Is the Mass a Sacrifice?" by Patrick McCloskey OFM (*Catholic Update*; St. Anthony Messenger Press).

The Truth About the Eucharist, by Fr. John Dowling (Liguori).

   Explains the doctrine of the Real Presence of Christ in the Eucharist.

Words Around the Table, by Gail Ramshaw (Liturgy Training Publications).

   Reflections on the words and symbols associated with the Eucharist.

Preparing for the Celebration

Read

"A true Christian is one who never for a moment forgets what God has done for us in Christ, and whose whole comportment and whole activity have their root in the sentiment of gratitude."

—John Baillie

Reflect

What signs of God's love in my life do I need to remember?

How does my daily life reflect my gratitude for God's love?

Pray

Dear Jesus, Son of the Father,
you made every minute of your earthly life an
   act of thanksgiving and praise.
Show me how to transform my life and touch
   the life of my child with that same gratitude.
Through the power of the Holy Spirit, may I be
   present to the world as a sign of God's love
   as you are present in the Eucharist.

Amen.

CHAPTER 7
SHARING THE BREAD OF LIFE
Pages 54–61

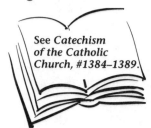

See *Catechism of the Catholic Church, #1384–1389.*

Background To show our respect for the presence of Jesus in the Eucharist, we follow certain rules and practices when it comes to receiving Holy Communion. "If you eat the bread and drink the wine in a way that isn't worthy of the Lord, you sin" (*1 Corinthians 11:27*). We reserve reception of Holy Communion, in most cases, to baptized Catholics—not because we want to contribute to the divided state of Christianity, but as a sign of the deep hunger we feel for real unity. We require confession and absolution of grave sin before receiving Communion—not because the Eucharist is reserved for perfect people, but out of the need to be reconciled with God and the community before accepting the invitation to the most intimate communion. We fast before Communion to remind ourselves of our hunger for the Bread of Life. But the most important Church rule with regard to the Eucharist is the duty and encouragement to receive Communion frequently, because that is how unity is built, sin conquered and our souls' true hunger fed.

Preparing Your Child at Home

Getting Started

- Review the bold-faced words, and clarify any that your child doesn't know or understand. If he or she hasn't yet learned the Lord's Prayer or the customary gestures used for the sign of peace, you will want to spend some time teaching them.
- Talk about the two photographs on pages 54 and 55. This chapter deals with receiving Holy Communion, so you might explain that the two photographs show the scene that leads up to the banquet. Pray together the opening prayer, and read the text on these pages.

Sharing the Scriptures

- Point out the bold-faced words, and review their meanings from within the text. Then read through the Scripture story on pages 56 and 57.
- Ask your child what scene he or she thinks the smaller framed picture is depicting (the Israelites gathering manna from the desert). Point out Jesus and his followers. Explain that when we share Jesus' Body and Blood in Holy Communion, we are receiving the food to help us live forever with God.

Exploring the Liturgy

- Review the bold-faced terms with your child. To describe the Eucharistic minister, you may wish to point to the woman offering the cup to the child. For the *We Ask* section, explain that the priest grants us *absolution* to symbolize God's forgiveness of the sins we have confessed.
- Read the text for "Holy Communion" and *We Ask* on pages 58 and 59. Review all three photos with your child, pointing out how the young girl on page 59 is cupping her hands and that those members of the congregation who are waiting to receive Communion are silent and respectful.
- *My Mass Book*—Allow your child time to complete pages 12–14. You may want to play some relaxing music for him or her. You can review the pages with your child either now or when you go through the chapter's *Sharing Page*. As you go through the pages, draw comparisons to your child's own experiences at Mass.

Living the Eucharist

- Read together the instructions to the exercise on page 60. Although you can't paste the photo yet, your child can write the expected date of his or her First Communion and draw a picture, if he or she wishes. Make a note to return to this page if your child chooses to use a photo.

- Read together the prayer on page 61, making the Sign of the Cross before and after. You may choose to read the text of the prayers and invite your child to join with you for the response. Explain to him or her that we join in this type of prayer after receiving Communion. Draw his or her attention to this moment during the next Mass you celebrate together.

More to Share

- Practice with your child the processional line and the receiving of Holy Communion. Explain what the priest will say and how we respond to him. You may be able to get unconsecrated Eucharistic bread from your church with which you can practice. Children are often curious how the host tastes and feels. You may also want to give your child a sip of wine. This will give them an idea of what to expect.
- Talk about what your child might pray during the silent time after Communion. Encourage your child to pray in his or her own words. Or have him or her memorize the Thanksgiving After Communion prayer found in the back of the child's book.
- *Sharing Page*—Complete the Chapter 7 *Sharing Page* together.
- Books and Videos—You may wish to share these additional resources, available from the library, your diocesan media center, or publishers' catalogs.

For children and families

Celebrating Eucharist with Children (8-part video series) (produced by Salt River Production Group; BROWN-ROA).

Segment 7: *Sharing the Bread of Life* is designed for use with this chapter.

Grandma's Bread (video) (Franciscan Communications/St. Anthony Messenger Press).

Mario learns about bread, First Communion, and the meaning of family.

The Greatest Table, by Michael J. Rosen (Harcourt Brace & Company).

Award-winning children's book artists illustrate this poem about a table that feeds the whole world.

The Unbeatable Bread, by Lyn Littlefield Hoopes (Dial Books for Young Readers).

In this parable Uncle Jon decides to bake a loaf of bread that will unite all creation.

For adults

Celebrating Eucharist with Families (2-part video series) (produced by Salt River Production Group; BROWN-ROA).

Father Joe Kempf helps adults explore the meaning of the Eucharist.

"Holy Communion from the Cup," by Leonard Foley OFM (*Catholic Update*; St. Anthony Messenger Press).

"Is the Mass a Meal?" by Charles Gusmer (*Catholic Update*; St. Anthony Messenger Press),

Preparing for the Celebration

Read

"The reality of our communion with Christ and in him with one another is the increase of love in our hearts."

—William Temple

Reflect

What does Holy Communion mean to me? How does my life give witness to my communion with Jesus and with others?

Pray

Jesus, Bread of Life,
sustain me with your presence
as I face the hungers of the world.
Welcome me always to the table
of the Eucharist. Help my child
feel welcomed, too.

Amen.

CHAPTER 8
GOING FORTH TO LOVE AND SERVE
Pages 62–69

See Catechism of the Catholic Church, #1402–1405.

Background The Eucharist, like all sacraments, is three-dimensional. At Mass we celebrate the memorial of Christ's Passion, recalling all salvation history. We celebrate Christ's presence with us in the here and now under the form of the sacred Bread and Wine. And we look to a future beyond all imagination—the heavenly banquet we will celebrate in the fullness of God's kingdom. As Christians with a baptismal mission, we participate fully in all three dimensions of the Eucharist. We are called to proclaim the good news of salvation history, to live as Christ's Body here and now, and to work and pray "in joyful hope" for the coming of the kingdom in fullness. "You are God's chosen and special people. You are a group of priests and a holy nation. God has brought you out of darkness into his marvelous light. Now you must tell all the wonderful things he has done" *(1 Peter 2:9)*.

Preparing Your Child at Home

Getting Started

- Ask your child to make up two missions. The first can be an imaginary, world-saving mission such as protecting the President. The other should be a mission that will benefit your household. It can be something as simple as taking out the trash or cleaning his or her room. Now talk with your child about how each mission is important. With each job people place their trust in you, so you owe it to them to do your best.
- Pray together the opening prayer, and read the text on pages 62 and 63.

- Ask your child what our mission is when we leave church (to pass on the message of God's love).

Sharing the Scriptures

- Ask your child to imagine what it would feel like if a best friend moved far away. Then ask how surprised your child would be to see that same friend walking down your street a few days later.
- Read together the story "In the Breaking of the Bread" on pages 64 and 65. Then, if possible, act out the story based on the text.
- Talk about what it felt like to be the main character of the story.

Exploring the Liturgy

- Read together the text on pages 66 and 67, including the *We Ask* question and answer.
- Look at the two photographs. Ask your child to remember when your pastor or deacon has dismissed you from Mass. Talk with your child about how this chapter might make him or her think differently about the end of Mass.
- *My Mass Book*—Allow your child time to complete pages 15 and 16. You may want to play some relaxing music for him or her. You can review the pages with your child either now or when you go through the chapter's *Sharing Page*. As you go through the pages, draw comparisons to your child's own experiences at Mass.

Living the Eucharist

- Read the directions to the "I Love and Serve" exercise on page 68. Allow time for your child to complete his or her candle design. Complete your own version, and when you've each finished, share your results.
- Read together the closing prayer on page 69. Begin and end with the Sign of the Cross. You may choose to read the text of the prayer and invite your child to join with you for the response. The next time you attend Mass together, draw your child's attention to the final blessing.

More to Share

- Now that your child has completed the preparation for First Communion, talk about how he or she is now better prepared to serve God in your family and in your community. Also, talk about what he or she would share with those who haven't yet gone through this preparation. How would your child help them prepare?
- *Sharing Page*—Complete the Chapter 8 *Sharing Page* together.
- Books and Videos—You may wish to share these additional resources, available from the library, your diocesan media center, or publishers' catalogs.

For children and families

Celebrating Eucharist with Children (8-part video series) (produced by Salt River Production Group; BROWN-ROA).

    Segment 8: Going Forth to Love and Serve is designed for use with this chapter.

To Dance with God: Family Ritual and Community Celebration, by Gertrud Mueller Nelson (Paulist Press).

    Suggestions for extending the liturgical celebration into the home and community.

Together with Jesus, We Build a Better World (St. Anthony Messenger Press).

    A prayer card with a meditation on living the Eucharist.

For adults

Liturgy: Becoming the Word of God (audio) (St. Anthony Messenger Press).

    Popular lecturer Megan McKenna discusses the integration of liturgy and life.

"Seven Ways to Enrich Faith-Life in Your Home," by Mitch Finley (*Catholic Update*; St. Anthony Messenger Press).

Preparing for the Celebration

In planning for your child's First Communion, remember to emphasize the liturgy as the most important part of the day.

Read

"If only we knew how to look at life as God sees it, we should realize that nothing is secular in the world, but that everything contributes to the building of the kingdom of God."

                —*Michel Quoist*

Reflect

How can I learn to look at life "as God sees it"? What is my own particular mission, the reason I have been sent?

Pray

Risen Jesus,
help me recognize you in every stranger
and remember that all the roads of my life
lead to Emmaus.
May my child and I know you always in the
breaking of the bread so that, nourished by
your word and your presence, we may joyfully
proclaim your kingdom.
Amen.

Catholic Prayers

These pages contain the texts of several traditional Catholic prayers. Refer your child to this section when you want to reinforce his or her familiarity with these prayers. Incorporate these prayers into the opening and closing prayers for each chapter.

The Sign of the Cross

- Always begin and end prayer time with the Sign of the Cross. If necessary, model for your child the traditional gesture of signing oneself with the cross.

- Have your child make the Sign of the Cross with holy water from the baptismal font or holy water container when he or she enters the church.

The Lord's Prayer

- Have your child suggest simple gestures to accompany the phrases of the prayer.

- Remind your child to listen for the Lord's Prayer at Mass and to join in praying it.

The Hail Mary

- Tell your child that this prayer to the mother of Jesus is part of many Catholic popular devotions.

Catholic Prayers

The Sign of the Cross

In the name of the Father,
and of the Son,
and of the Holy Spirit.
Amen.

The Lord's Prayer

Our Father, who art in heaven,
hallowed be thy name;
thy kingdom come;
thy will be done on earth as it is in heaven.
Give us this day our daily bread;
and forgive us our trespasses
as we forgive those who trespass against us;
and lead us not into temptation,
but deliver us from evil.
Amen.

Hail Mary

Hail, Mary, full of grace,
the Lord is with you!
Blessed are you among women,
and blessed is the fruit of your womb, Jesus.
Holy Mary, Mother of God,
pray for us sinners,
now and at the hour of our death.
Amen.

70 : Catholic Prayers

Background

The Sign of the Cross Tracing the cross on one's own body or the forehead of another has been a common Christian gesture since the early centuries of the Church. The words of this traditional prayer echo the Rite of Baptism.

The Lord's Prayer This prayer has its roots in Scripture. In the Gospels of Matthew **(Matthew 6:9–13)** and Luke **(Luke 11:2–4)**, Jesus teaches a form of this prayer to his disciples. In various forms, this prayer is used by all Christians. The Lord's Prayer is prayed at Mass, in communal celebrations of the Sacrament of Reconciliation, and as part of the Rosary.

The Hail Mary The first part of this prayer was used as an antiphon in the Little Office of Our Lady, a form of the Liturgy of the Hours prayed during the Middle Ages. The antiphon combines the Archangel Gabriel's greeting at the annunciation **(Luke 1:26–28)** with Elizabeth's words of praise for Mary's motherhood **(Luke 1:42)**. The second part of the prayer was added as devotion to Mary grew.

Catechetical Background

For more on the significance of the Lord's Prayer in Christian spirituality, see the *Catechism of the Catholic Church (#2777–2865)*.

Glory to the Father (Doxology)

Glory to the Father,
and to the Son,
and to the Holy Spirit,
as it was in the beginning,
is now, and will be for ever.
Amen.

Blessing Before First Communion

May the Lord Jesus touch your ears to receive his word,
and your mouth to proclaim his faith.
May you come with joy to his supper
to the praise and glory of God.
Amen.

Prayer Before Communion

How holy is this feast
in which Christ is our food:
his passion is recalled,
grace fills our hearts,
and we receive a pledge of the glory to come.

—based on a prayer of Thomas Aquinas

Thanksgiving After Communion

Lord our God,
we honor the memory of Saint Pius X
and all your saints
by sharing the bread of heaven.
May it strengthen our faith
and unite us in your love.
We ask this in the name of Jesus the Lord.
Amen.

Catholic Prayers : 71

Glory to the Father (Doxology)

- Explain to your child that *doxology* means "words of praise." This ancient prayer praises God, the Holy Trinity.
- Teach your child a sung version of this prayer, the hymn "Praise God from Whom All Blessings Flow." Explain that "Holy Ghost" is an old English way of saying "Holy Spirit."

Blessing Before First Communion

Use this prayer just before your child's First Communion Mass. You or a family member may wish to trace a small cross on your child's ears and mouth as you mention those words in the blessing.

Prayer Before Communion

Have your child memorize this prayer and pray it at Mass.

Thanksgiving After Communion

Encourage your child to pray this prayer quietly after receiving Communion.

Background

Glory to the Father The first three lines of this praise of the Trinity originated in the Eastern Church. In the fourth century the last lines were added, and the prayer was in common use in both the East and the West by the fifth century. It is part of the Rosary and is traditionally used to conclude the praying or chanting of a psalm in the Liturgy of the Hours.

Blessing Before First Communion Blessing, or invoking God's presence and favor on a person, place, or thing, is an ancient custom of the Church. The practice of parents blessing their children was popular among the peoples of Old Testament times as well.

Prayer Before Communion This prayer, traditionally prayed during the fast before Communion, is adapted from a longer Eucharistic hymn attributed to Saint Thomas Aquinas, the medieval doctor of the Church who wrote several such hymns.

Thanksgiving After Communion This prayer is based on the Communion prayer for the Feast of Saint Pius X, from the Sacramentary. Tell children that Saint Pius X was pope at the beginning of the twentieth century. He changed Church rules so that children as young as seven years old could receive Holy Communion.

The Life of Jesus

These pages remind your child of some of the important events in Jesus' life. Refer to these pages to help your child put Scripture stories and doctrinal points about Jesus' life in context.

- Review this material with your child at least once during the course of his or her preparation for First Communion.
- Have your child choose particular events to act out or illustrate.
- Share with your child illustrated Bible storybooks that tell the story of Jesus' life.

The Life of Jesus

Here are some of the important events in Jesus' life as they are described in the Gospels.

The Annunciation
God sent the Angel Gabriel to tell Mary she was going to be the mother of Jesus, God's own Son.

The Nativity
Jesus was born in Bethlehem in a shelter for animals. Angels told shepherds the good news that the Savior was born.

The Presentation
At the Temple in Jerusalem, Mary and Joseph offered a sacrifice of thanksgiving for Jesus' birth. Simeon and Anna, two prophets, recognized Jesus as the Messiah.

The Epiphany
Wise teachers from faraway lands came to worship Jesus.

The Escape to Egypt
An angry king threatened to kill Jesus. Joseph, his foster father, was warned in a dream to take Mary and Jesus to Egypt.

The Young Jesus in the Temple
On a trip to Jerusalem for the Passover, Jesus became separated from Mary and Joseph. They looked for him and found him in the Temple, talking about God's word with wise teachers.

Jesus' Baptism by John
When Jesus was about thirty years old, he began his public life of teaching. He was baptized in the Jordan River by his cousin John, a prophet.

The Temptation in the Desert
After his baptism Jesus went alone to the desert to pray and fast. He was tempted by Satan, but he remained true to God, his Father.

Jesus Calls the Apostles
Jesus gathered a group of special friends and helpers called the apostles. Other men and women also followed Jesus and helped him in his work.

Scripture Background

Here are some Scripture references for the events listed on these pages:

The Annunciation—*Luke 1:26–38*
The Nativity—*Matthew 1:18–25; Luke 2:1–20*
The Presentation—*Luke 2:22–40*
The Epiphany—*Matthew 2:1–12*
The Escape to Egypt—*Matthew 2:13–15*
The Young Jesus in the Temple—*Luke 2:41–52*
Jesus' Baptism by John—*Matthew 3:13–17*
The Temptation in the Desert—*Matthew 4:1–11*
Jesus Calls the Apostles—*Matthew 4:18–25; Mark 2:13–15; Luke 6:12–16; John 1:43–51*
Jesus Teaches—*Matthew 5:1—7:29; Mark 4:1–34; Luke 10:25–37; Luke 15:11—17:10; John 6:22–59; John 10:7–18*
Jesus Heals—*Matthew 15:29–31; Mark 5:21–43; Luke 7:1–10, 36–50; John 5:1–15; John 8:1–11*
Jesus Shows God's Love—*Luke 7:11–17; John 2:1–12; John 6:1–15; John 11:1–44*
Jesus Enters Jerusalem—*Matthew 21:1–11*
The Last Supper—*Luke 22:7–23; John 13:1—14:31*
In the Garden—*Mark 14:32–52*
The Trial—*Matthew 26:57—27:30*
The Crucifixion—*Luke 23:26–49; John 19:16–37*
The Burial—*John 19:38–42*
The Resurrection—*Matthew 28:1–10; Mark 16:1–8; Luke 24:1–12; John 20:1–18*
The Ascension—*Acts 1:6–11*

Jesus Teaches

Jesus taught crowds of people about God's love. He told stories called parables.

Jesus Heals

In the name of God, his Father, Jesus healed people who were sick or troubled. He forgave sins.

Jesus Shows God's Love

Jesus worked miracles, or powerful signs of God's love. He changed water into wine at a marriage feast. He fed thousands of people with only a little food. He brought people who were dead back to life.

Jesus Enters Jerusalem

After about three years of teaching, Jesus entered Jerusalem for the Passover. He knew he faced death because certain leaders were angry with him. Some people, waving palm branches, welcomed Jesus as a king as he rode into the city.

The Last Supper

On the night before he died, Jesus celebrated the Passover meal with his friends. He washed their feet as a sign that they should serve others. He shared himself with them in the first Eucharist.

In the Garden

After supper Jesus went to a garden with his friends to pray. One of his friends betrayed him by turning Jesus over to the leaders who wanted to kill him. Jesus was arrested and taken to jail.

The Trial

Jesus was accused of acting against the law. He was whipped and beaten. The leaders sentenced Jesus to death.

The Crucifixion

Jesus was executed by being nailed to a cross. While he hung on the cross, he forgave those who had sentenced him. Then Jesus died.

The Burial

Jesus' body was taken to a tomb. The tomb was sealed with a large stone.

The Resurrection

On the third day after Jesus' death, God the Father raised him to new life. When Jesus' friends visited his tomb, they found the stone removed and the tomb empty. Later Jesus himself appeared to them in glory.

The Ascension

Forty days after the resurrection, Jesus returned to his Father in heaven. Jesus promised to send the Holy Spirit to teach and guide the Church.

The Life of Jesus : 73

Note the following feasts and holy days that celebrate events in the life of Jesus by marking the dates on a family calendar or helping your child make charts listing them.

- The Solemnity of the Annunciation—March 25
- The Feast of the Nativity (Christmas)—December 25 (holy day)
- The Solemnity of the Presentation—February 2
- The Feast of the Epiphany—Sunday closest to January 6
- The Temptation in the Desert—recalled in the 40 days of Lent
- Jesus Enters Jerusalem—celebrated on Passion (Palm) Sunday, the Sunday before Easter
- The Last Supper—celebrated on Holy Thursday, the Thursday before Easter
- The Crucifixion—recalled on Good Friday, the Friday before Easter
- The Solemnity of the Resurrection—celebrated at the Easter Vigil and on Easter Sunday, the Sunday after the first full moon of spring
- The Feast of the Ascension—celebrated on Ascension Thursday, 40 days after Easter (holy day)

Art Background

All three paintings featured on these pages were produced in a style loosely described as "folk art." The figures are simplified, classical notions of perspective are discarded, and bright colors predominate. The childlikeness of this art is not due to a lack of skill or maturity, but to the willingness to see the world as a child does, uncomplicated by sophisticated art theories.

- *The Adoration of the Magi*, by L. Powell, shows the exotic nature of the visitors by using highly decorative colors and patterns.
- Jessie Coates, the African American painter of *Last Supper*, is sometimes called an "outsider artist." This category of folk art includes artists who, intentionally or otherwise, break out of the stereotyped notions of art to reveal challenging truths.
- William H. Johnson, painter of *Mount Calvary*, was a founder of the Harlem Community Art Center. A classically trained artist who lived and worked in Europe, Johnson later simplified his style in a conscious attempt to reflect the African American folk spirit.

Holy Communion

Receiving Holy Communion

Review these rules and practices with your child as part of his or her preparation for First Communion.

- Explain to your child that although all followers of Jesus are part of the Body of Christ, not all Christians share our belief in the Real Presence of Jesus in the Eucharist. We pray that all Christians will one day be united, but until that time we do not share at the table of the Eucharist.

- Review with your child the definitions of mortal and venial sin. Remind him or her that through the reception of Communion venial sins are forgiven.

- Explain that *fasting* means going without food or drink, with the exception of water or medicine.

- Catholics have a duty to receive Communion at least once a year, preferably during the Easter Season, which extends from Easter through Trinity Sunday. But encourage your child to receive Communion frequently.

- Catholics may receive Communion more than once a day, if the second time is also within a Mass.

Holy Communion

Receiving Holy Communion

Catholics follow these rules and practices to show respect for the Eucharist:

- Only baptized Catholics may receive Communion.
- To receive Holy Communion, we must be free from mortal sin. We must be sorry for any venial sins committed since the last time we celebrated the Sacrament of Reconciliation. When we have contrition, receiving Holy Communion frees us from venial sin.

- To honor the Lord, we fast for one hour before receiving Communion. We go without food or drink, except water or medicine.
- Catholics are required to receive Holy Communion at least once a year, if possible during Easter time. But we are encouraged to receive Communion every time we participate in the Mass.
- Catholics are permitted to receive Communion at a second Mass on the same day.

Background

Receiving Holy Communion   These rules for receiving Holy Communion are based on canon law. Although Eucharistic practice has varied throughout the years, the Church today emphasizes the importance of frequent Communion in strengthening our union with Christ and with one another.

Catechetical Background

For more on the significance of Holy Communion, see the *Catechism of the Catholic Church* (#1382–1405).

Handling sensitive topics   For any number of reasons, family members of children receiving First Communion may not themselves be receiving Communion. Be sure to explain to your child that people should never be judged on whether or not they receive Communion.Those who are not receiving Communion may simply come forward and cross their arms over their chests as a sign that they wish to receive a blessing instead.

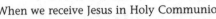

How to Receive Communion

When we receive Jesus in Holy Communion, we welcome him with our whole bodies, minds, and spirits.

Here are steps to follow when you receive Communion:

- Fold your hands, and join in singing the Communion hymn as you walk to the altar.

- When it is your turn, you can receive the consecrated Host in your hand or on your tongue. To receive it in your hand, hold your hands out with the palms up. Place one hand underneath the other, and cup your hands slightly. To receive the Host on your tongue, fold your hands, and open your mouth, putting your tongue out.

- The priest or Eucharistic minister says, "The Body of Christ," and you answer, "Amen." The priest or minister places the Host in your hand or on your tongue.

- Step aside and stop. If you have received the Host in your hand, carefully take it from your palm, and put it in your mouth. Chew and swallow the Host.

- You may also be offered Communion from the cup. After swallowing the Host, walk to where the cup is offered. The deacon or Eucharistic minister says, "The Blood of Christ." You answer, "Amen."

- Take the cup from the priest, deacon, or minister. Take a small sip, and carefully hand the cup back.

- Quietly return to your place. Pray a prayer of thanksgiving.

Holy Communion : 75

How to Receive Communion

Refer to this material when providing proximate preparation for First Communion.

- Review these steps with your child before and during First Communion practices.

- Provide any additional information about how Communion is distributed in your parish, such as directions for coming forward and returning to one's place in an orderly fashion. This is especially important if your parish's usual custom involves kneeling for Communion, receiving the host on the tongue, or other practices not in general use.

- If possible, practice using unconsecrated hosts or Eucharistic bread and wine, so your child will become familiar with the taste. Your child may need more than one practice to feel comfortable handling the cup.

Illustrated Glossary of the Mass

This section gives a visual reference for the people, places, and things associated with the Eucharistic celebration.

- Throughout your child's preparation for First Communion, refer to this section to enhance his or her understanding of the Mass.

- Invite your child to draw his or her own illustrations for each of the terms.

- Take your child on a tour of the parish church. Ask the sacristan or another parish minister to show your child some of the sacred vessels and vestments used by your parish community.

- Go through the glossary word by word, asking your child to tell when and how each item is used or what each minister does.

Illustrated Glossary of the Mass

altar
(AWL•ter): The table of the Eucharist. At the altar the sacrifice of the Mass is offered to God.

ambo
(AM•boh): The lectern, or reading stand, from which the Scriptures are proclaimed. The ambo is sometimes called "the table of the word."

assembly
(uh•SEM•blee): The community gathered to celebrate the Eucharist or another sacramental liturgy.

baptismal font
(bap•TIZ•muhl FAHNT): The bowl-shaped container or pool of water used for Baptism. The word *font* means "fountain."

Book of the Gospels
(BUK uhv thuh GAHS•puhlz): A decorated book containing the readings from the four Gospels used during the Liturgy of the Word.

Catechetical Background

For more on the people, places, and things associated with the celebration of the Eucharistic liturgy, see the *Catechism of the Catholic Church* (#1135–1186).

cantor

(KAN•ter): The minister who leads the singing at Mass and during other Church celebrations.

chalice

(CHA•luhs): The special cup used at Mass to hold the wine that becomes the Blood of Christ.

ciborium

(suh•BOHR•ee•uhm): A container for hosts. A ciborium may hold the smaller consecrated Hosts used for Communion. A covered ciborium also holds the Blessed Sacrament in the tabernacle.

cruets

(KROO•uhts): Small pitchers or containers for the water and wine used at Mass. Many parishes use larger pitchers to hold the wine, especially if people will be receiving Communion from the cup.

deacon

(DEE•kuhn): A man who is ordained to serve the Church by baptizing, proclaiming the gospel, preaching, assisting the priest at Mass, witnessing marriages, and doing works of charity.

Eucharist

(YOO•kuh•ruhst): The sacrament of Jesus' presence under the form of sacred Bread and Wine. We receive Jesus' own Body and Blood as Holy Communion during the Eucharistic celebration, the Mass. The word *Eucharist* means "thanksgiving."

host

(HOHST): A round piece of unleavened bread used at Mass. When the host is consecrated, it becomes the Body and Blood of Christ. We receive the consecrated Host in Holy Communion.

incense

(IN•sents): Oils and spices that are burned to make sweet-smelling smoke. At Mass and in other liturgical celebrations, incense is sometimes used to show honor for holy things and as a sign of our prayers rising to God.

Lectionary

(LEK•shuh•nair•ee): The book of the Scripture readings used at Mass.

lector

(LEK•ter): A minister who proclaims God's word at Mass or during other liturgical celebrations. The word *lector* means "reader."

offering

(AW•fuh•ring): The gifts we give at Mass. Members of the assembly bring our offering of bread and wine to the altar. We also give an offering of money, called a *collection*, to support the work of the Church.

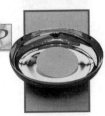

paten

(PA•tuhn): The plate or dish used at Mass to hold the bread that will become the Body and Blood of Christ.

priest

(PREEST): A man who is ordained to serve God and the Church by celebrating the sacraments, preaching, and presiding at Mass.

Sacramentary

(sa•kruh•MEN•tair•ee): The book of prayers used by the priest at Mass. Another name for this book is the **missal** (MIH•suhl). Members of the assembly may use booklets called **missalettes** (mih•suh•LETS) to follow the readings and join in the responses and prayers.

sanctuary

(SANGK•chuh•wair•ee): The part of the church where the altar and the ambo are located. The word *sanctuary* means "holy place."

Glossary : 79

server
(SER•ver): A minister, usually a young person, who helps the priest and deacon at Mass. An older person who carries out this ministry is known as an **acolyte** (A•koh•lyt).

tabernacle
(TA•buhr•na•kuhl): The box, chest, or container in which the Blessed Sacrament is reserved, or kept. The tabernacle may be placed in the sanctuary or in a special Eucharistic chapel or area. A lamp or candle is kept burning near the tabernacle as a sign that Jesus is present. The word *tabernacle* means "meeting place."

usher
(UH•sher): A minister of hospitality who welcomes members of the assembly to Mass and helps direct processions and collections.

vestments
(VEST•muhnts): The special clothing worn by the priest and some other ministers for Mass and other liturgical celebrations. The priest wears an **alb** (ALB), **chasuble** (CHA•zuh•buhl), and **stole** (STOHL). The deacon wears a **dalmatic** (dal•MA•tik) or an alb and a stole. The colors of vestments usually indicate the season of the liturgical year.

wine
(WYN): A drink made from grape juice that has fermented. At Mass the consecrated Wine becomes the Body and Blood of Christ. We may receive the consecrated Wine from the cup at Communion.

Belonging

Family Note

We Are Invited We talked about how we belong to different groups and how members of a group share their time and talents. Your child learned that he or she became a member of the Church at Baptism and that belonging to the Church means being a follower of Jesus Christ—in other words, being a **Christian**.

We Remember We shared the story of **Pentecost**. We talked about how Peter and the other apostles received the **Holy Spirit** and shared the good news of Jesus' life, death, and resurrection with the people of Jerusalem. Afterward, many of these people chose to be baptized and to share in the life of the Church (*Acts 2*).

We Celebrate Your child learned that we become a part of the Church through Baptism and Confirmation, two of the **Sacraments of Initiation**. Through Baptism, which we celebrate with water and holy words, we become members of the Church. Through Confirmation, in which we are **anointed** with oil and receive the laying on of hands, our faith is strengthened.

Living the Eucharist

- Share a story of when a new member joined your family through birth, adoption, or marriage. Talk about how that person was welcomed and how he or she has participated in your family's life.

- Talk with your child about ways of welcoming new members to groups he or she belongs to.

- Talk together about why you belong to the Church. Share your feelings about how being a part of the Church has influenced your actions at different times in your life.

- Review the story of Pentecost. Help your child imagine what it would have felt like to have been in the crowd who listened to the apostles.

- Ask your child to share with you the cross he or she filled in. Be sure to discuss why belonging to Jesus and the Church is important to your child.

- The symbol chosen for this chapter is the baptismal font. Decorate or enhance the picture on the other side of this page, or copy the symbol onto the material of your choice. Use the picture of the font to begin a First Eucharist mosaic or banner you will construct with your child.

Family Prayer
Pray together.

> We belong to one another as a family whether we're together or apart. We also belong to God's family. Help us, God the Father, Son, and Holy Spirit, always remember to pray for one another. We give thanks to you and ask your blessing on all families. Amen.

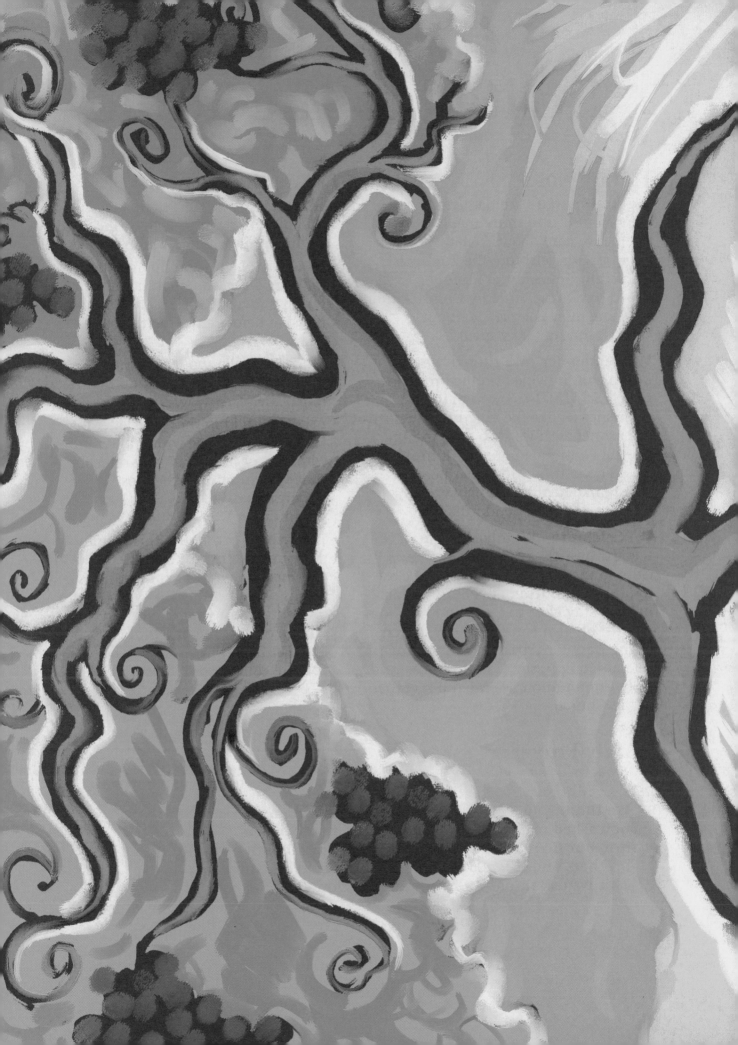

Invited to the Table

Family Note

We Are Invited   We discussed how important it is to share meals with people we care about. When we meet for Mass, we celebrate the **Eucharist**. We receive Jesus in the form of sacred Bread and Wine. In **Holy Communion** we share more completely in our Church family's holy meal.

We Remember   We shared the parable of the vine and the branches (*John 15:1–17*). Jesus said that he nourishes us like the vine nourishes the branches. If we stay close to him, we will continue to grow in faith. As we do good things for other people, we are like healthy branches that produce plenty of good fruit.

We Celebrate   We talked about how, like the branches that need to stay close to the vine, we need to stay close to Jesus. The Sacraments of Initiation help us stay close to Jesus and help join us with other members of the Church in the **Body of Christ**. When we have celebrated Baptism, Confirmation, and Holy Communion, we are full members of the Church.

Living the Eucharist

- Talk together about family meals and about how it feels to be included in the family's conversation.

- As a way of showing appreciation for each other, together make your family's favorite foods. Say a special blessing before enjoying the meal.

- Review the story of the vine and the branches. Talk about how members of your family need one another in much the same way.

- Ask your child to share the letter to Jesus that he or she wrote. Talk further with him or her about why receiving Holy Communion is the most important part of his or her First Communion Day.

- The symbol chosen for this chapter is the vine and its branches. Decorate or enhance the picture on the other side of this page, or copy the symbol onto the material of your choice. Add the picture of the vine and branches to the First Eucharist mosaic or banner you are constructing together.

Family Prayer

Pray together.

> We thank you, O God our Father, for inviting us to be nourished with your love. Teach us to invite others into our hearts and lives. May we one day sit with our brothers and sisters at the banquet of life everlasting. This we ask through Christ our Lord. Amen.

Gathering to Celebrate

Family Note

We Are Invited   We talked about how we like to share our celebrations with members of our **community** and how we share the celebration of the Eucharist with our Church community, or parish.

We Remember   Your child learned that the early Church community met in each other's homes to celebrate and remember Jesus. We also talked about how the early Christians shared money, prayers, and talents within their faith community (*Acts 2:42–47*).

We Celebrate   Your child learned that when we enter the church, we remember our Baptism by making the Sign of the Cross. The Mass begins with the prayers and actions that make up the **Introductory Rites**. We begin with a **hymn** and a **procession**. We also talked about how Jesus is present in the priest who leads us, called the **presider**, and in the **assembly**, the people who gather to celebrate Mass together.

Living the Eucharist

- Talk with your child about family events that make you happy. Encourage your child to talk about his or her favorite family times.

- Review the story of the early Christian community with your child. Talk about why others would look at the Christians as models of love.

- The next time you attend Mass together, make a special point of greeting the people around you.

- Go through pages 1–4 of *My Mass Book* together. Help your child learn the responses for the Introductory Rites.

- The symbol chosen for this chapter is the processional cross and banner. Decorate or enhance the picture on the other side of this page, or copy the symbol onto the material of your choice. Add the picture of the cross and banner to the First Eucharist mosaic or banner you are constructing together.

Family Prayer
Pray together.

> **God our Father, we gather together to praise and thank you. We are nourished by your friendship, caring, forgiveness, and understanding. With one heart and voice, we celebrate with you through Christ our Lord. Amen.**

Feasting on God's Word

Family Note

We Are Invited   We talked about stories that we like to hear and share. Stories help us learn about the world and understand people better. Your child learned that we hear the stories of God's love in the **Scriptures** and that we read from Scripture as part of the Mass.

We Remember   We shared the story of the Good Shepherd. Jesus told this story so that people would understand that God loves and protects them as a shepherd looks after his sheep (*John 10:1–18*).

We Celebrate   Your child learned about the **Liturgy of the Word**, the part of the Mass when we listen to readings from the Bible, and about the **psalm** we pray or sing between the first and second readings. The third reading, the **gospel**—which literally means "good news"—tells us about Jesus' life and teachings. To show how happy we are to hear the news, we say "**Alleluia!**" before the gospel is read. After the gospel the priest gives a **homily** to help us understand the readings and apply them to our lives. Then we pray the **Creed** to express our Christian beliefs.

Living the Eucharist

- Talk with your child about stories and books that you have enjoyed. Find out about his or her favorite stories.

- Begin a family stories notebook. Write down stories told by family members. Ask your child to make illustrations for the stories.

- Share your favorite Bible story with your child, or take turns reading stories from the Bible. Ask your child to share the Bible story he or she wrote about or illustrated.

- Go through pages 5–7 of *My Mass Book* together. Help your child learn the Creed and the other responses used during the Liturgy of the Word.

- The symbol chosen for this chapter is an ambo. Decorate or enhance the picture on the other side of this page, or copy the symbol onto the material of your choice. Add the picture of the ambo to the First Eucharist mosaic or banner you are constructing together.

Family Prayer
Pray together.

> Lord God, we bless and thank you for giving us your Word, Jesus, to show us the way to you. May we be open to your message of love always and proclaim it in Jesus' name. Amen.

Offering Our Gifts

Family Note

We Are Invited   We talked about how people often bring gifts to special meals. When the Catholic family shares its special meal at Mass, we offer the gifts of ourselves and of bread and wine. We also share gifts of money to support the parish and to help people who are in need.

We Remember   We read the story in which Jesus fed five thousand people with only five loaves of bread and two fish *(John 6:5–13)*. This story reminds us of Jesus sharing himself with us in the Eucharist.

We Celebrate   Your child learned that the second great part of the Mass is called the **Liturgy of the Eucharist**, during which Jesus comes to us in Holy Communion. We discussed the **presentation of gifts**, in which our gifts of bread and wine are taken to the **altar**. During the **collection** we share our money with the Church and with those less fortunate than ourselves.

Living the Eucharist

- Talk with your child about how to share his or her talents and treasure with the community. Ask to see your child's writing or artwork that shows how he or she would like to share.

- Review the story of the loaves and the fish. Talk with your child about how a boy's small gift helped many people.

- If your parish has a program for families to carry up the gifts during a weekend Mass, volunteer to take part in that program.

- Go through page 8 of *My Mass Book* together. Help your child learn the responses during the presentation of gifts.

- The symbol chosen for this chapter is a basket with loaves and fish. Decorate or enhance the picture on the other side of this page, or copy the symbol onto the material of your choice. Add the picture of the loaves and fish to the First Eucharist mosaic or banner you are constructing together.

Family Prayer

Pray together.

> **God our Father, we give you thanks for the gifts you have given us—for eyes to see with, ears to hear with, and hands that may do your work.**

Continue this prayer by naming other gifts from God.

Conclude with: **We praise you in Jesus' name. Amen.**

Remembering and Giving Thanks

Family Note

We Are Invited We talked about Thanksgiving customs and the things we are thankful for. Your child was reminded that **Eucharist** means "thanksgiving" and that at every Mass we give thanks to God our Father for sending us the gift of Jesus.

We Remember We shared the story of the Israelites' Passover from slavery into freedom (the *Book of Exodus* in the Bible) and the story of Jesus' Last Supper (a Passover meal), during which he instituted the Eucharist by sharing his body and blood in the form of bread and wine *(Matthew 26:17–19, 26–28).*

We Celebrate Your child learned about the Eucharistic Prayer, the great prayer of the Mass in which we give thanks and praise to God. During the Eucharistic Prayer the bread and wine are **consecrated** by the power of the Holy Spirit as the priest speaks Jesus' words from the Last Supper.

Family Prayer

Pray together.

> We give thanks to you, Lord. Your love is everlasting and your works are wonderful. You satisfy those who are thirsty and fill the hungry with good things. Jesus, you are our nourishment now and forever. Amen.

Living the Eucharist

- Talk together about the things your family thanks God for. Have your child share his or her writing or drawing from class.

- When you say grace or pray a meal blessing, let family members take turns praying prayers of thanksgiving in their own words.

- Share a family story of God's love, forgiveness, or liberation as the Jewish people do each year at the Passover feast.

- Go through pages 9–11 of *My Mass Book* together. Help your child learn the "Holy, Holy, Holy Lord" and the memorial acclamation.

- The symbol chosen for this chapter is the altar. Decorate or enhance the picture on the other side of this page, or copy the symbol onto the material of your choice. Add the altar picture to the First Eucharist mosaic or banner you are constructing together.

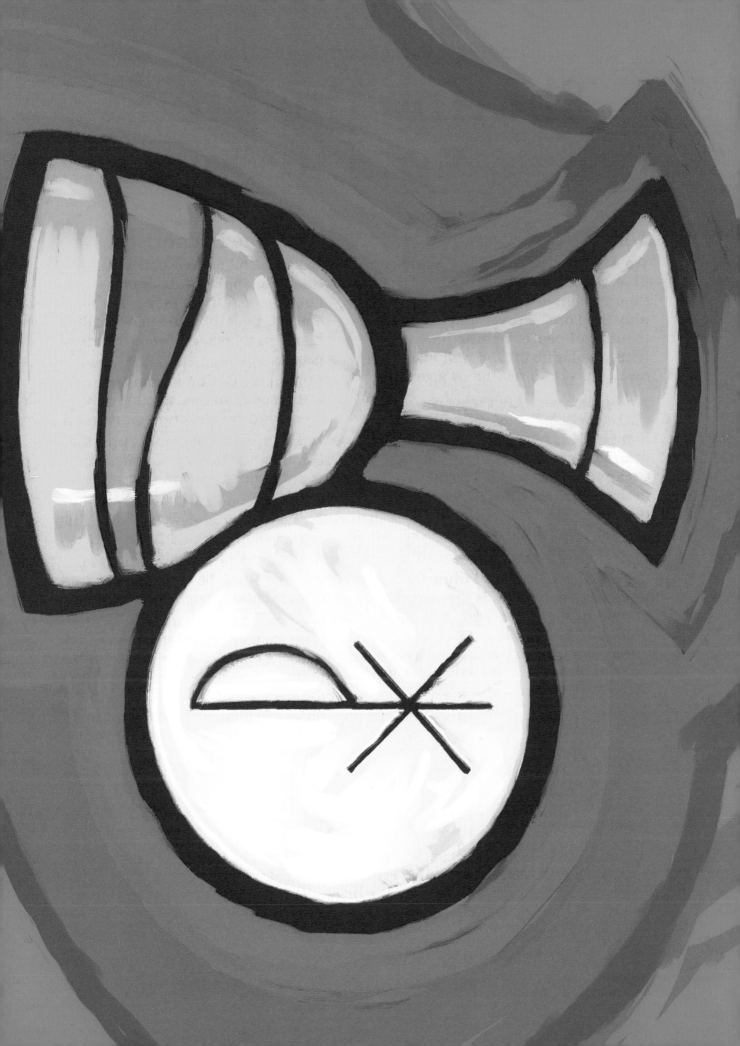

Sharing the Bread of Life

Family Note

We Are Invited   We talked about how we celebrate the banquet of Holy Communion at Mass. To prepare, we pray the **Lord's Prayer** and exchange the **sign of peace**. We also pray that Jesus, the **Lamb of God**, will take away our sins and bring us peace.

We Remember   After Jesus performed the **miracle** of the loaves and fish, he reminded his followers about the **manna**, or bread from heaven, that God had sent to feed his people living in the desert. We also shared Jesus' teachings about how Communion will bring us eternal life *(John 6:30–58)*.

We Celebrate   We talked about how the priest or **Eucharistic minister** gives us Communion. We receive the Communion Host in our hands and drink from the cup of consecrated Wine. After we receive Communion, we show our thanks by praying or by singing a Communion song.

Living the Eucharist

- Tell your child about how you feel when you make peace after a disagreement. Help him or her see opportunities for making peace at home, in school, and with friends.

- Review with your child the proper way to receive Communion. Share with your child any special prayers you say after receiving Communion.

- Talk with your child about how the Lord's Prayer helps you understand your relationship with God.

- Go through pages 12–14 of *My Mass Book* together. Review with your child the Lord's Prayer and Lamb of God.

- At a later date you may want to paste on page 60 of the textbook a picture of your child's First Communion.

- The symbol chosen for this chapter is the chalice and host. Decorate or enhance the picture on the other side of this page, or copy the symbol onto the material of your choice. Add the picture of the chalice and host to the First Eucharist mosaic or banner you are constructing together.

© BROWN-ROA

Family Prayer

Pray together.

> Lord Jesus Christ, you are the Bread of Life. Provide for our needs today. Help us care especially for those who have less than we do. We pray the prayer you taught us.

Join hands and pray the Lord's Prayer.

Going Forth to Love and Serve

Family Note

We Are Invited We talked about how important it is to be sent on a **mission**. When the priest dismisses us from Mass, he sends us to carry on the work of Jesus and spread the news of God's love.

We Remember We shared the story of the two followers of Jesus who met him on the road between Jerusalem and Emmaus on the first Easter *(Luke 24:13–35)*. These followers joyfully shared the news of the **Messiah's** resurrection.

We Celebrate We talked about how going to Mass and receiving Communion bring us closer to God and one another. As we are dismissed, we are sent out into the world "to love and serve the Lord." Because we are made stronger when we participate in the Mass, we are better able to see Jesus in other people and are encouraged to let others see Jesus in us.

Living the Eucharist

- Talk with your child about other people you know who do God's work in the world. Anyone who helps people live in peace and find God in one another is doing God's work.

- Review the story of Jesus and his followers on the road to Emmaus. Talk with your child about how it must have felt to see Jesus after the resurrection.

- Talk with your child about ways your family can "love and serve the Lord." Ask your child to share his or her list of things to do to share God's love.

- Go through pages 15 and 16 of *My Mass Book* together. Help your child learn the responses to the Closing Rite.

- The symbol chosen for this chapter is a pair of hands breaking and sharing the bread. Decorate or enhance the picture on the other side of this page, or copy the symbol onto the material of your choice. Add the picture of the hands breaking and sharing bread to complete the First Eucharist mosaic or banner you are constructing together.

Family Prayer
Pray together.

God our Father, through the example of your Son, Jesus, you show us how to love and care for those who are poor, hungry, and oppressed. Teach us to lessen the suffering of our brothers and sisters around the world. We ask this in Jesus' name. Amen.